Prayers around the Crib

Juliette Levivier

Illustrations by Anne Gravier

CTS Children's Books

Table of Contents

Advent

Prepare a way for the Lord,
make his paths straight.

It will be Christmas soon !

In four weeks' time we'll be celebrating the birth of Jesus. These four weeks are called Advent. 'Advent' means arrival. Someone we are waiting for is coming.

We have to get ready for Jesus' coming. We have to decorate the house and buy presents of course, but above all we have to get our hearts ready.

There's no time to lose ! What do I have to change in my life so I can welcome Jesus better ?

Lord Jesus,
I want to prepare
myself to receive you
in joy and peace.
Light up the path
that leads me to
Christmas.
Amen.

5

The Advent calendar

My soul is waiting for the Lord.

Psalm 129:5

It seems a very long time till Christmas !

It's really hard to be patient when there are Christmas trees and adverts for toys everywhere.

A nice Advent calendar can help you prepare for Christmas: you can open one of the windows every day.

These windows are the windows of your heart. You open them one by one to let the light of God shine into you. Even if some days your heart stays closed like a shuttered window, the light of the Lord doesn't go out.

Lord, teach me to live peacefully
one day at a time,
not wanting everything right now,
and help me to keep trying.
Help me to stay faithful
to my daily prayer. Amen.

The Christmas tree

*I tell you most solemnly, anyone who
believes has eternal life.*

John 6:47

There are Christmas trees everywhere; at school, in
the streets, in the shops, even in church !
But do you know why we have Christmas trees ?
These trees are evergreens. They are a symbol of life
because they stay green even in the depths of winter !
We put them in our homes and decorate them to
remind ourselves that with Jesus we live forever.

It's great fun to go with Dad or Mum and buy a tree
and to take it home and decorate it !
I want to put the lights on it so that it shines at night.
I want to decorate it with baubles that are round like
the earth, because Christmas is for the whole world.

Lord God, I give you thanks
for the life you have given us.
With your help I want to love
my life and look after it.
I want to live
forever with you.
Amen.

The Advent wreath

You will be a crown of splendour
in the hand of the Lord.

Isaiah 62:3

At Christmas, Jesus drives the shadows away.
He brings us the light. He is the Light.

One beautiful Advent custom is to have a wreath
made of fir tree branches and decorated with four
big candles.

We light one of these candles on each of the four
Sundays of Advent. They symbolise the light of
Christmas that is coming and the darkness of winter
that is disappearing bit by bit.

What can I do so I can better receive the light of
Christmas ? How can I too be a light which lights up
the way of the Lord ?

Round like the earth,
green like hope: Lord, how
beautiful your crown is,
shining in the night!
Truly, you are the
King of the Universe.
Amen.

Mistletoe and holly

*I am like a vine putting out graceful
shoots, my blossoms bear the fruit
of glory and wealth.*

Sirach 24:17

Isn't holly lovely with its prickly shiny leaves ? Its red
berries liven up winter. The wreath of holly on every
front door reminds me of Christ's crown of thorns.
All the little red berries between the prickly holly
leaves show me that life has triumphed over death.

Mistletoe looks so delicate ! This plant with its
nice white berries grows on the branches of trees
and feeds on their sap. I feed on the sap of the tree
that shelters me, too. That tree is Jesus ! He feeds
me with his word and with the Eucharist.

You think of everything, Lord !
The plants that liven up
our winter are so beautiful !
In spite of the cold, in spite of the snow,
they tell us that life is still there,
and that hope is stronger than suffering.
They tell me I can bear fruit
throughout my life.
Amen.

The crib

She gave birth to a son, her first-born.
She wrapped him in swaddling clothes
and laid him in a manger
because there was no room for them at the inn.

Luke 2:7

The crib is the name of the simple place where
Mary laid her baby, Jesus. For a long time,
Christians have put cribs in their homes to remind
themselves of this. Cribs are made up of little
figures of Jesus, Mary, Joseph and a crowd of others.

Each year we wrap them up carefully in tissue paper
and put them away in their box. It's as if they are
sleeping. It makes us very happy when we take them
out again – it's time to wake them up - and set up a
beautiful crib ! My heart needs to wake up, too !
I need to be ready when Jesus comes.

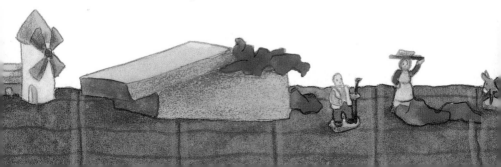

I am ready to welcome you too, Lord.
My parents, my brothers and sisters,
my friends, my neighbours and I –
we make up a joyful crowd
coming to adore you.
Keep us all united to each other.
Amen.

15

The donkey

*Joseph set out from the town of Nazareth
in Galilee for Judaea, to David's town
called Bethlehem, since he was of
David's house and line.*

Luke 2:4

The donkey that carried Mary from Nazareth to Bethlehem was lying on the straw. It was happy to be resting. It had travelled a long way. It was hot and thirsty. It had carried a heavy load but had walked on bravely. Joseph's kind voice and Mary's gentle touch had helped it on its way...

Sometimes people say donkeys are stubborn or stupid. It's true that this donkey didn't understand much, but it was gentle and brave, and was happy to serve.

Sometimes I'm asked to do difficult things too, but I can try my best to help.

Lord, there's a place in your Church for
everyone. Everyone can be a servant.
Everyone has talents they can bring.
Everyone is important.
Teach me not to despise anyone
but to recognise each person's qualities.
Amen.

The ox

And here is a sign for you: you will find
a baby wrapped in swaddling clothes
and lying in a manger.

Luke 2:12

The ox was lying quietly in its byre when suddenly a
tired couple and their donkey arrived. Then a baby
started crying. Where had they come from ? Next
there was the gentle song of a mother cradling her
newborn baby: "Alleluia ! The Lord has done marvels
for me."

Then there were even more strangers: angels,
shepherds, sheep ! What a lot of people ! How
unexpected ! The good beast was happy to welcome
them. He was happy to share his humble home.

Now let me also try to welcome people who come
and bother me.

Leaning over you, Jesus,
the ox warmed you with his gentle breath.
Like him, by the breath of the Holy Spirit,
I can spread the warmth of your peace
and love around me.
Amen.

Mary

Mary gave birth to her first-born son.

Luke 2:7

Mary is the one who says 'yes'. She was open to what God asked of her on the day of the Annunciation. Here she is now, ready to welcome Jesus, her tiny baby.

20 In the crib, she is usually put in the place of honour on Jesus's right. Kneeling before him, in silent wonder, she represents all the mothers of the world.

Do I know how to rest in silent wonder at the presence of Jesus within me ?

Blessed are you, Mary !
You are really blessed among all women !
By your 'yes', Jesus came to live among us.
Teach me to say 'yes' each day of my life.
Amen.

Joseph

*When Joseph woke he did what the
angel of the Lord had told him to do.*

Matthew 1:24

Standing near Mary, Joseph prays and keeps watch. He doesn't speak much. Like all the fathers of the world who are present with him in front of Jesus, he watches over the child. Joseph leans on God and trustingly obeys him.

I don't always like to obey ! Obeying God means letting yourself be loved and responding to that love. It means accepting his plan of love for you. We get close to God by obeying his Word and his Church. Truly, obedience is wonderful !

Lord, I too want to come to you
in silence and offer you my life.
I want to pray in silence,
without speaking,
just contemplating you,
letting myself be guided,
letting myself be loved,
so every day of my life
I may do what you ask of me.
Amen.

Christmas –
Jesus is born !

She will give birth to a son and you must name him Jesus, because he is the one who is to save his people from their sins.

Matthew 1:21

Jesus is born. The name 'Jesus' means 'God saves'. He is also called 'Emmanuel' which means 'God with us'. Jesus, Emmanuel - it's the same thing ! It's God coming to you and me.

I put him in the centre of the crib. All the other figures are turned towards him.

Let's look at him, adore him, stay close to him. May we be filled with his presence.

A child is born.
He is our God.
He is our Saviour.
Alleluia !

Christmas –
Jesus comes to save us

Here is your God... he is coming to save you.

Isaiah 35:4

Christmas is a great feast that reminds us of
Jesus's birth, Jesus the Son of God made man.
It's like a birthday... with more than 2000 candles !
The present is Jesus himself ! He brings us the love
of God. He comes to save us from sin and death.
He is the Saviour the world has been waiting for,
for so long.

I've been waiting a long time too ! Four whole weeks.
That's a long time ! Today it's wonderful to celebrate
with Jesus and rejoice with all those I love.

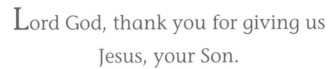

Lord God, thank you for giving us
Jesus, your Son.
He is your Word.
He is your love.
He comes to give us his life,
to give us true Life !
Amen.

Jesus will come again in glory

They will see the Son of Man coming on the clouds of heaven with power and great glory.

Matthew 24:30

Christmas time comes every year. The Advent wreath reminds me that Jesus will also come again. Advent is not just waiting for Christmas, but also waiting for Jesus to return.

Jesus will come again in glory, not as a poor and weak baby, but with all the majesty and power of a king. His reign will have no end. He will be king for all eternity.

To save me,
you came as a tiny baby;
you died on the cross;
you rose again.
When you come again on the clouds,
you will see how I have tried to love you
in all my words and actions.
Amen.

29

The angels

See, I bring you news of great joy, a joy to be shared by the whole people. Today in the town of David a Saviour has been born to you;
he is Christ the Lord.

Luke 2:10-11

How noisy these angels are ! With all their songs and trumpets, they're going to end up waking the baby Jesus... No, he's still sleeping peacefully. The shepherds are astounded by these joyful messengers.

The angels give glory to God. They sing of his marvels and teach us to praise him.

Singing is beautiful ! They say "singing is praying twice". So I won't hesitate to join my voice with the angels, singing and praising God.

Blessed are you, Lord, for the angels !
They sing of your glory without end.
They sing your praise without end !
I want to sing with them:
'Glory to God in the Highest.'
Amen.

The shepherds

*They hurried away and found Mary and Joseph,
and the child lying in the manger.*

Luke 2:16

The poor shepherds were terrified. They rubbed
their eyes. They couldn't believe their ears.

"Where have all these angels come from ? What's
this great joy they're announcing ? A Saviour ?
Born this evening ? Unbelievable !" Astonished and a
bit worried, they hurried off to see Jesus. These poor
simple shepherds were the first to visit him...

When they left they were very happy and told
everyone they met what they had heard and seen.
Great joy like this needs to be shared...

I haven't seen Jesus, but I know he is the Son of
God and I can witness to his love.

Lord, you see that I am only a child
but you came down from heaven
for little children and for
the humble and lowly !
You came for me.
You came to save me.
Thank you for giving me
peace and joy this Christmas.
Amen.

The sheep

*The Lord is my shepherd; there is nothing
I shall want. Fresh and green are the pastures where
he gives me repose.*

Psalm 23:1-2

Almost all sheep are white - they are like people who
are pure in heart. They came to Jesus with trust.

The sheep came with all that they had - just their
wool for knitting into little socks to keep a baby's
feet warm !

I too am like a sheep. Jesus is my shepherd ! He
guides me and leads me. He looks for me when I am
lost.

Let me bring to the crib all that I am and all that I
have. It's nothing extraordinary. But for God I am
special because I am his child !

Lord, you are my shepherd !
Protect me from evil and from sin.
Show me the way of joy and peace.
Lead me to happiness,
the happiness of living with you forever.
Amen.

The man who is overwhelmed with joy

Blessed are the pure in heart; they shall see God.

Matthew 5:8

In some countries there is always another figure in the crib. He is overwhelmed by what he has just discovered. He is standing there with his arms wide open. He is still wearing a night cap because he has just got out of bed and he is running to see Jesus. He has a simple heart and he is rejoicing at Jesus's birth. He has nothing to give Jesus except his heart which is full of love. But isn't that the best gift of all ?

Am I ready to welcome Jesus with all my heart ?

I don't have a lot to offer him either. Maybe I have nothing to offer at all ? But wait a minute: I can offer him my joy and my smile and my care for others and all the little things I do out of love !

Give me a pure and simple heart,
a joyful heart, open to your love,
overwhelmed by your wonders !
Open my heart to your presence,
open my heart to my brothers and sisters.
I only have my heart to offer you, Lord,
but I give every bit of it to you !
Amen.

The miller

Give us each day our daily bread.

Luke 11:3

Often there is another figure in the crib: the miller, dressed in his best clothes and with a cotton hat on his head. He is carrying a large sack of flour on his shoulder to give to Jesus. The flour represents all his work. With his flour, you could make enough bread to feed everyone there.

Bread is a very good thing ! Jesus himself is the Bread of Life. He feeds my soul and gives me Life.

Like the miller, I can offer my work to Jesus. My schoolwork, my efforts, the progress I make, my good marks and my bad marks... And why not the work of announcing the Good News of the Gospel as well ?

Lord, you invite me to your table.
When I share in the bread of the Eucharist
with my brothers and sisters,
it is you Lord who come to me.
You give yourself to me.
You are present in me.
Thank you Lord.
Amen.

The other figures

Great numbers who had heard what he was doing, came to him.

Mark 3:8

You can put many other figures in the crib. They can represent the people of God, all those throughout history who, beginning with Abraham, have been waiting for the Messiah. They also represent all the people who have ever seen that Jesus is their Saviour.

What a lot of people ! And yet, Jesus knows each one by name. He loves each one with a special love.

I'm just like a little figure in the crib too. But Jesus sees me and knows me. He calls me to live with him forever ! My name too is written in heaven !

Lord, so many people
are looking for the truth.
So many people
are looking for you.
Reveal your love
to all the peoples of the earth,
so they can give you glory together. 41
Amen.

The star

*We saw his star as it rose and we have
come to do him homage.*

Matthew 2:2

The stars are so beautiful, so mysterious and far
away. They shine at night to guide travellers and fill
the sky with their light.

The star which guided the kings to Jesus shone
so brightly that they couldn't stop themselves from
following it. They didn't really know where it was
leading them but they put their trust in it !

Jesus is the light which shines for all men and guides
them to God. Could I be like a star, showing others
the path that leads to Jesus ?

Lord, be my star.
When I am in the dark,
when my heart is darkened
by doubt, sadness and sin,
be the light shining before me !
Amen.

The three Kings

*They saw the child with his mother, Mary,
and falling to their knees they did him homage.*

Matthew 2:11

Aren't the Kings handsome ! Aren't they majestic
with their presents and their jewels ! Aren't their
clothes colourful !

They've come from so far away, they've taken so
much trouble, they've left everything to see Jesus
and give him praise. They are so great and he is so
small... But there they are, Kneeling in front of Jesus;
they Know that he is the King of Kings.

They invite me to set off on a journey too, to leave
everything and go to meet Jesus. But where will I
find, gold, frankincense and myrrh ?

Lord Jesus, the kings bow down
before you even though
you are just a little baby...
But you too are a King !
You are the King of the universe.
You are the King of my heart.
I come to kneel down before you.
Amen.

O come all ye faithful

O come all ye faithful
Joyful and triumphant,
O come ye, O come ye to Bethlehem.
Come and behold Him
Born the King of Angels.

O come let us adore Him (x 3)
Christ the Lord.

God of God, Light of Light,
Lo, he abhors not the Virgin's womb.
Very God, begotten not created.

See how the shepherds,
Summoned to His cradle,
Leaving their flocks, draw nigh to gaze.
We too will thither
Bend our joyful footsteps.

Lo! star-led chieftains,
Magi, Christ adoring,
Offer Him incense, gold, and myrrh.
We to the Christ Child bring our hearts' oblations.

Splendour Immortal,
Son of God Eternal,
Now hidden in mortal flesh our eyes shall view.
See there the Infant, swaddling clothes enfold him.

Child, for us sinners
Poor and in the manger,
We would embrace Thee, with love and awe.
Who would not love Thee, loving us so dearly ?

Sing! Choirs of Angels;
Sing in exaltation,
Sing, all ye citizens of heaven above;
Glory to God, in the highest.

Yea, Lord, we greet thee !
Born this happy morning,
Jesus, to Thee be glory given;
Word of the Father,
Now in flesh appearing:

CTS Children's Books

The Bible for little children, *by Maïte Roche*
(ISBN 1 86082 399 8 CTS Code CH 2)

The Gospel for little children, *by Maïte Roche*
(ISBN 1 86082 400 5 CTS Code CH 1)

The Rosary, *by Juliette Levivier*
(ISBN 1 86082 397 1 CTS Code CH 3)

The Way of the Cross, *by Juliette Levivier*
(ISBN 1 86082 398 X CTS Code CH 4)

First prayers for little children, *by Maïte Roche*
(ISBN 978 1 86082 443 2 CTS Code CH 5)

Praying with the friends of Jesus, *by Juliette Levivier*
(ISBN 978 1 86082 444 9 CTS Code CH 6)

Prayers around the Crib, *by Juliette Levivier*
(ISBN 978 1 86082 445 6 CTS Code CH 7)

The most beautiful Christmas Story, *by Maïte Roche*
(ISBN 978 1 86082 446 3 CTS Code CH 8)

Faith for children, *by Christine Pedotti*
(ISBN 978 1 86082 447 0 CTS Code CH 9)

Prayers around the Crib: Published 2007 by the Incorporated Catholic Truth Society, 40-46 Harleyford Road, London SE11 5AY. Tel: 020 7640 0042; Fax: 020 7640 0046; www.cts-online.org.uk. Copyright © 2007 The Incorporated Catholic Truth Society in this English-language edition.

ISBN: 978 1 86082 445 6   CTS Code CH 7

Prier autour de la crèche by Juliette Levivier, illustrations by Anne Gravier, published 2006 by Edifa-Mame, 15-27 rue Moussorgski, 75018 Paris; ISBN Edifa 978-2-9145-8093-9; ISBN Mame 978-2-7289-1193-6. Copyright © Groupe Fleurus 2006.